3/93

D0754722

SAM WALTON

The Giant
of
Wal-Mart

Anne Canadeo

 GARRETT EDUCATIONAL CORPORATION

Cover: *Sam Walton.* (Photography by Zavell Smith, San Antonio, Texas.)

Manufactured in the United States of America

Edited and produced by Synthegraphics Corporation

Library of Congress Cataloging-in-Publication Data

Canadeo, Anne, 1955-
   Sam Walton, the giant of Wal-Mart / Anne Canadeo.
     p. cm. — (Wizards of business)
   Includes index.
   Summary: A biography of Samuel M. Walton, whose ingenuity and persistence contributed to his becoming one of the wealthiest men in America.
   ISBN 1-56074-025-6
   1. Walton, Sam, 1918-   —Juvenile literature.   2. Businessmen—United States—Biography—Juvenile literature.   3. Millionaires—United States—Biography—Juvenile literature.   4. Wal-Mart (Firm)—History—Juvenile literature.   [1. Walton, Sam, 1918-
2. Businessmen.   3. Wal-Mart (Firm)—History.]   I. Title.
II. Series.
HC102.5.W35C36   1991
381′.149′092—dc20   91-32776
[B]   CIP
                                                 AC

921
walton

Contents

Chronology for **Sam Walton**

1918	Born on March 29 in Kingfisher, Oklahoma
1936	Graduated from Hickman High School in Columbia, Missouri
1940	Graduated from the University of Missouri
1940–1941	Worked at J.C. Penney in Des Moines, Iowa, as a management trainee
1942	Entered the U.S. Army
1943	Married Helen Robson on February 14
1945	Opened first Ben Franklin variety store in Newport, Arkansas
1950	Lost lease on Newport store; opened first "Walton's 5¢ & 10¢" in Bentonville, Arkansas
1962	First Wal-Mart opened in Rogers, Arkansas
1970	Wal-Mart went public
1974	Retired as chairman and chief executive officer
1976	Returned as chairman and chief executive officer
1982	Diagnosed with hairy cell leukemia
1983	First Sam's Wholesale Club opened in a suburb of Oklahoma City, Oklahoma
1984	Instituted "Buy American" campaign
1985–1989	Named "Richest Man in America" by *Forbes* magazine
1987	First Hypermart USA opened in Garland, Texas
1988	First Wal-Mart Supercenter opened in Washington, Missouri
1989	Diagnosed with bone cancer
1990	Approximately 1,500 discount and wholesale Wal-Mart outlets did $25.8 billion in sales

Chapter 1

Pioneer Stock

In the late 1950s, a crazy new fad swept across the country. It was fun, inexpensive, and everybody wanted to try it. What was it? The hula hoop, of course.

Samuel Moore Walton knew that he could sell hundreds of hoops at the **variety stores** he owned in Bentonville and other small towns in Arkansas. (Terms in **boldface type** are defined in the Glossary at the back of this book.) The problem for Sam—and many other owners of small stores—was getting enough hula hoops from **distributors**. Large stores were favored and their orders filled first. Small stores had to make do with leftovers—and miss out on the big **profits**.

SOLVING A PROBLEM

Sam Walton, however, was not one to miss the chance to sell such a hot item. Ever innovative and enterprising, Sam sat down with a hula hoop and considered his problem.

"What is a hula hoop, after all?" Sam asked himself. Nothing more than a length of plastic tube, bent in a circle and joined at the ends. Sam decided that if he couldn't get distributors to supply him with enough hula hoops, he'd find a way to make his own.

He located a factory in nearby Siloam Springs, Arkansas, that made plastic tubing. Then he enlisted the help of another store owner named Jim Dodson. Dodson was Sam's competitor, but the two store owners were on good terms and both needed hula hoops.

As partners, Walton and Dodson bought the plastic tubing and went to work at night, happily making as many hoops as they could sell. "It was a brilliant idea," Dodson later said. "We'd make several thousand a night. Sam would haul his off and spread 'em around his stores."

While other small storekeepers moaned about missing out on the hula-hoop fad, the enterprising Sam Walton had cleverly—and profitably—solved his problem.

The hula-hoop episode was a very small moment in Walton's extraordinary career, but the story clearly illustrates his ingenuity, persistence, and amazing ability to figure out a way around almost any roadblock between himself and a goal. They are certainly traits that contributed to making Walton one of the wealthiest men in America. If ever the motto "Where there's a will, there's a way" applied to a man, that man is Samuel M. Walton, who comes from a family of pioneers.

PIONEER HERITAGE

Sam Walton's ancestors came to the United States from England. They settled first in Virginia, then moved on to Missouri. J.W. Walton, one of Sam's ancestors, was a sheriff in Webster County,

Missouri. In 1889, J.W. decided to move farther west, to Kingfisher, Oklahoma, in hopes of making a better life for his family.

Back in Webster County, J.W.'s brother Samuel, who was Sam's grandfather, ran a general store. J.W. urged Samuel to come to Oklahoma, but the prosperous shopkeeper had little reason to leave Missouri.

Samuel's daughter Mollie, however, was tempted to go west by Uncle J.W.'s grand stories about Kingfisher. Although quite young, she became a schoolteacher within two years after arriving in Oklahoma. Mollie was earning thirty-five dollars a month when she received news of her father's death. She immediately sent for her three younger half-brothers—Earl, Freeman, and Thomas.

Tom Walton

Despite Mollie's youth, she raised her half-brothers as though they were her own children. Uncle J.W. and his family helped. Since moving to Kingfisher, J.W. had developed a good business as a land agent. He determined the value of farms and arranged **mortgages**. When Tom, Mollie's youngest half-brother, was finished with school, Uncle J.W. took him into the business.

While traveling around the countryside, Tom met a young woman named Nancy Lee Lawrence, whose family had come to Oklahoma from Kansas. Tom soon proposed to the pretty, shy, eighteen-year-old Nan, and they were married in 1917.

Tom and Nan moved into a farmhouse a few miles out of town. When their first child was born on March 29, 1918, Tom decided to name the boy after his own father, Samuel Moore Walton. A second son was born in 1921. Although he was named James, everyone called him Bud.

HARD TIMES

The mid-1920s were hard times for Oklahoma farmers. Grain prices were so low that they could not make enough money to cover their expenses. Because the farmers around Kingfisher were having such a difficult time, Tom Walton was not doing well with his farm mortgage business. To earn a better living, he decided to move his family to a new town.

Tom, Nan, and the two boys returned to Missouri. There, Tom went to work for his oldest half-brother, who, like Uncle J.W. back in Kingfisher, also ran a farm mortgage company. For the next ten years, the family moved from town to town in Missouri, living in Springfield, Marshall, and Shelbina.

The Great Depression

Tom Walton worked hard, driving an average of 100 miles each day to do his job. However, because the entire country was now in the grips of the **Great Depression**, his efforts barely kept the family finances afloat.

But Tom was a Walton, and like all Waltons, he was innovative, persistent, and optimistic. As he drove around the countryside, he developed a talent for trading for family necessities. He also taught his sons to work hard, and to be ambitious and thrifty.

SHELBINA'S FIRST EAGLE SCOUT

Sam, Tom's oldest son, was close to his father and worked hard to please him. He earned pocket money by doing odd jobs—painting a neighbor's porch or bottling the extra milk from the family cow and selling it. "Work, work, *work*! That's the only way to get ahead," Sam's father drummed into his son's head, and Sam did.

Soft-spoken and shy, Sam was surprisingly a natural leader and very popular in school. He was an excellent student and also a good athlete. At Shelbina High School, Sam played halfback on the football team, which was undefeated in his sophomore year. At age fifteen, he was also the first Boy Scout in Shelbina's history to become an Eagle Scout, the highest honor in scouting.

Local Hero

To qualify for Eagle Scout, Sam needed to earn at least twenty-one merit badges and also demonstrate that he could save a life, either by first aid or rescue. Sam did it the hard way—by actually saving someone's life.

It happened while Sam was on a picnic with his class along the banks of the Salt River. It had rained heavily that spring and the river was swollen, the current fast and deep. A boy named Donald Peterson fell into the river and was in danger of drowning. Sam acted quickly, jumping into the water and pulling Donald to safety. Soon after, he was awarded scouting's highest honor.

In the summer of 1933, when Sam was fifteen, his family moved once again. This time it was to Columbia, Missouri, which was larger than Shelbina. Because the University of Missouri and some other smaller colleges were located there, Sam's mother was pleased about that part of the move. She wanted both of her children to get a college education, and hoped that Sam would become a lawyer.

"Most Versatile Boy"

Some boys might have had a hard time adjusting to a new school (Hickman High School) in a more sophisticated town, but Sam Walton took the change in stride. He made friends easily and continued to excel in both academic and athletic activities. One former classmate describes him as " . . . a hard worker. He was optimistic all the time. He had a great smile on his face and felt like everybody was his friend and the world was something he could conquer."

Sam was even more enterprising in Columbia at his odd jobs than he had been in Shelbina. He got up early in the morning to deliver the *Columbia Missourian*, a newspaper put out by the University of Missouri's journalism students. Significantly, he also took a part-time job in a local five-and-ten-cent store.

At high school, Sam played on the basketball and football teams, took part in many clubs, and was elected president of the student body in his senior year. In the school yearbook, the caption under Sam's picture read, "Most Versatile Boy."

COLLEGE DAYS

Just as his mother wanted, Sam enrolled at the University of Missouri after graduating from high school in 1936. The Waltons' economic picture was improving, but Sam still had to work his way through college. His paper route had grown to over 160 subscribers, and for several years straight, he was the newspaper's top salesman. He also waited tables at the college in exchange for meals and worked as a lifeguard in the summers at the town swimming pool.

This picture of Sam Walton was taken in 1985, almost 50 years after his graduation from high school. Now one of America's richest men, Sam is seen here meeting with employees at a new Wal-Mart in Conway, Arkansas. (Jim Knowles/Picture Group.)

Somehow, Sam still found time to take an active part in a fraternity at college, teach Sunday school, serve as president of his senior class, and do so well in his studies that he was elected to an exclusive honor society upon graduation. An article about Sam, published in his college fraternity newspaper during his senior year, was aptly titled, "Hustler Walton."

Everyone who knew Sam Walton could see that this bright, engaging, industrious young man had all the qualities necessary for success in the years to come. However, just what remarkable heights he'd reach, no one could possibly predict.

Chapter 2

The Penney Days

Upon Sam's graduation from the University of Missouri in 1940 with a degree in economics, the bright campus star and "hustler" faced a world with many doors open to him.

However, the celebratory mood of his graduation was shadowed by sad news from his parents. After more than twenty years of marriage, Tom and Nan decided to separate. Nan moved to St. Louis, Missouri, and Tom moved to Fulton, Missouri, a short distance from Columbia.

At the time, World War II had started in Europe. For the past four years, Sam had trained in the U.S. Army Reserve, in the artillery. He knew that some day he would be called up to serve, but it was impossible to say when. While waiting, Sam began a new phase of his life with a different, but very important kind of "training."

GETTING INTO RETAILING

All through college, the father of Sam's steady girlfriend had urged him to enter the field of insurance. Sam seriously considered the idea. But he thought that in order to be a success in insurance, he would have to take graduate courses. However, Sam didn't have any money for graduate school, and he was impatient to begin a full-time career.

During Sam's senior year at college, representatives of Sears, Roebuck and J.C. Penney had been on campus interviewing students for jobs. Sam liked what he heard about the **retail** business and went to St. Louis, where the Penney headquarters were located, to meet with the company's general manager.

The J.C. Penney Company offered Sam a job as a management trainee at eighty-five dollars a month. Sam was delighted with the opportunity and told his brother Bud to apply, too, which he did. Bud began working for Penney's in Cedar Rapids, Iowa, while Sam was sent to their store in Des Moines, Iowa, where he quickly learned the J.C. Penney retailing philosophy.

The Penney Philosophy

John Cash Penney had begun his department store chain in the early 1900s. He was still very active in the business in his late sixties, when Sam Walton worked in the Des Moines store. Penney would frequently visit the stores, watch the performance of his salespeople, and take time to have a personal word with each of his employees. He once watched Sam conduct a sale and later showed him how to wrap a package without wasting paper.

It could be said that, in many ways, Sam Walton modeled

himself after John Cash Penney. He certainly learned a lot about retailing during the time he was in Des Moines. He also learned a basic business philosophy that deeply impressed him.

In 1940, J.C. Penney operated 1,586 stores in smaller towns and cities, and did about $300 million a year in sales. One of Sam's first assignments as a trainee was to memorize the seven tenets (principles) of the "Penney Idea." The basis of these tenets was to put customer satisfaction above profit and to reward workers in the organization for their efforts.

Learning How to Raise Money

J.C. Penney called his employees "associates"—a term that Walton would later borrow and use in his own company. Penney had begun using the term when he needed to raise capital to expand. He would invite his managers to invest in new stores and become his partners. Not surprisingly, when Walton later wanted to expand his chain of five-and-ten-cent stores, he used the same method of raising capital with manager-partners.

Sam worked at Penney's for about eighteen months, absorbing retailing lessons that remained with him for a lifetime. But knowing that he would soon have to serve in the Army, he moved from Des Moines to Claremore, Oklahoma, so he could be closer to home. Sam took a temporary job in a gunpowder factory in Claremore.

A FATEFUL MEETING

The paths of Helen Robson and Sam Walton had probably crisscrossed several times while they both attended college in Columbia, Missouri. While Helen took her first two years at Christian College,

Sam was finishing his last two years at the University of Missouri. But they had never met.

Helen graduated from the University of Oklahoma in 1941 with a degree in economics. She then returned to her hometown of Claremore, where she worked in her father's law office and also did the bookkeeping for the family ranch.

Helen and Sam finally met at a bowling alley in Claremore one spring night in 1942. Sam noticed a strikingly pretty, dark-haired girl bowling a few lanes over. With his typical friendly charm, he walked over and said, "Don't I know you?"

Helen replied first with a smile. They both knew that they had never met before. But wartime had made eligible bachelors scarce in Claremore—especially young men as handsome as Sam. Looking him squarely in the eye, Helen said, "You do now."

The Town's "Best Catch"

Sam had no way of knowing at the time that he had just introduced himself to a girl who was probably the "best catch" in Claremore. Helen was pretty, smart, and quite athletic. She was also an accomplished musician who played the bassoon and piano.

Helen's family was quite wealthy, especially for that post-Depression era, but Helen was not spoiled. As classmates described her, ". . . she didn't act like a rich girl."

Helen's father, L.S. Robson, had taught his children the value of a dollar and thrifty ways. He had started out so poor that he had to sell Bibles and cookware in order to earn his way through law school. Until his practice got rolling, he even took in typing for ten cents a page.

Robson's law practice eventually grew, and he later became

involved in banking, which built his fortune. In 1929, he bought over 18,000 acres of Oklahoma pasture land and started a cattle ranch.

To young Sam Walton, L.S. Robson must have seemed the very essence of the "American Dream" and all that Sam aspired to. In later years, Robson would help Sam get a start in business and would provide him with valuable advice.

A Whirlwind Courtship

Helen recalls that soon after meeting Sam, they began to date almost every night. Their romance went quite smoothly, until a girl from Des Moines named Beth Hamquist came to Claremore for a visit.

While Sam worked at J.C. Penney, he had dated Beth, who was a store cashier. But because it was against company policy for Penney employees to date each other, Sam and Beth had to carry on their relationship in secret. (Oddly enough, even though Sam broke the rules back then, he was to adopt much the same rule for his own company.)

Beth hoped that she and Sam would marry and had come to Claremore to convince him to do so. Sam, however, had other ideas. In fact, one of the reasons he had left Des Moines was to put some distance between himself and marriage-minded Beth. Sam was now forced to make his feelings clear.

Helen also had a chance to marry another fellow. Looking back on her choice to marry Sam, she once told a reporter, "I thought life with him would be so interesting."

Army and Marriage

Soon after Beth left Claremore, Sam and Helen became engaged. Sam was then called into the Army in July of 1942. However, a minor physical problem made him ineligible to be sent overseas.

Helen and Sam were married on Valentine's Day, February 14, 1943. They set up their first household in Salt Lake City, Utah, where Sam was assigned as a captain of a military police battalion.

Their first child, a son, was born on October 28, 1944, in Tulsa, Oklahoma. Sam and Helen combined family names for the boy, whom they called Samuel Robson Walton, or Rob for short.

AN IMPORTANT QUESTION

Sam Walton was discharged from the Army in August of 1945. The war in Europe was over, although fighting continued in the Pacific, where Bud was serving as a pilot of a Navy torpedo bomber.

With his wife and baby, Sam frequently visited with the Robsons in Claremore. For some fun, L.S. Robson would take Sam out quail hunting and taught him what he knew. The hobby turned out to be one of Sam's great pleasures. "My father-in-law was a great quail hunter and a tremendous trainer of dogs," Sam once told a friend. "When I got out of the Army, he took me bird hunting. I was hooked, just hooked!"

Although bird hunting was a fascinating enjoyment, Sam couldn't avoid facing an important question: What to do with his life next? The temporary stint of "working" for Uncle Sam was over, and he was eager to get started on his business career.

Chapter 3

Off to a Great Start in Newport

In 1945, the small farming town of Newport, Arkansas, did not exactly appear to be on the verge of a postwar boom. Located ninety miles northeast of Little Rock, Arkansas, the town had been founded in 1835. With both the White River and the Black River close by, Newport was a busy stop for steamboats for a time. But steamboat commerce ended when the railroads moved in during the late 1800s.

THE RIGHT PLACE

When Sam Walton and his family first set foot in Newport, the town had a population of only 4,000. Local farmers raised cotton, corn, and rice.

18

During the war, many people had left Newport and other such small towns to seek work in factories on the West Coast or in large cities of the Midwest, like Detroit and Chicago. Newport industry consisted largely of a shoe factory and a metal mill.

All in all, Newport was an unlikely starting point for a man who was to become a millionaire . . . and then a billionaire. To Sam Walton, however, Newport looked like just the right place for his first business enterprise.

Buying a Franchise

The **franchise** for a Ben Franklin five-and-ten-cent store on one of Newport's busiest corners was for sale. Sam looked over the deal, the store, and the town. He quickly decided he wanted to buy the franchise.

The Ben Franklin variety stores were controlled by the Butler Brothers Company of Chicago. There were over 2,000 stores in the chain, most located in rural towns too small to attract the larger Woolworth or Kresge stores. Each was owned and operated under an individual franchise.

The Butler Brothers supplied a manual to franchise owners about how to operate a Ben Franklin store. It explained just about everything a person needed to know about the five-and-ten-cent store business.

Goods for a store could be bought at **wholesale** prices from the Ben Franklin warehouse in St. Louis. A store owner did not have to buy items only from the Butler Brothers. However, it was hard for the owner of small store to buy in quantities large enough to beat the Butler Brothers' prices.

Walton immediately liked the idea of having his own store.

He arranged to borrow $25,000 from his father-in-law and bought the franchise, a deal which included all **merchandise** and fixtures. The rental was $200 dollars a month, or five percent of the **gross profits**. The store was 50 by 120 feet, a large space in those days before giant supermarkets and **discount** stores.

Twenty-seven years old and only a few months out of the Army, Sam Walton was suddenly the owner of his first store. It was a proud and happy day.

SMALL TOWN ADVANTAGES

Life in Newport appealed to both Sam and Helen for many reasons. They felt comfortable with the people who lived there and quickly made friends. When their neighbors said Sam and Helen were "as common as anybody," it was a great compliment to the newcomers.

Sam became very active in civic affairs. As president of the Newport Chamber of Commerce, he worked to bring new business to the town. Helen was active in the church, charity organizations, and social clubs. They both liked to hike, canoe, and camp in the nearby forests of the beautiful Ozark Mountains. Much to Sam's unending delight, the countryside around Newport was a great place for quail hunting.

Although Sam worked long hours in his new store, he would often take a break to drive out to the country with his gun and first bird dog, Peggy. Hunting was his favorite hobby now, and his dogs were quite important to him.

Sam would have many dogs throughout his lifetime, but one named Old Roy was undoubtedly his favorite. When this faithful hunting companion died, Sam put Old Roy's picture on the label of Wal-Mart brand dog food.

Raising a Family

The Waltons thought Newport was a nice place in which to raise a family. They bought a small white house and, in the fall of 1946, Helen had their second son, John. A third boy, named James, was born in the summer of 1948.

At the time of James' baptism, Sam's parents, Tom and Nancy, came to Newport for a visit. Sam was pleased to see that they were no longer living apart. In 1949, Sam and Helen had a girl, their fourth child, whom they named Alice.

Sam was out of the house from early morning until after the children had gone to bed. Helen recalls that she was left with most of the day-to-day responsibilities for raising their four children. However, Sam still found time to attend his childrens' school plays or other activities. He also served as a Boy Scout leader and took the children on hiking and camping trips or to lakeside vacations. He and Helen also took them to church every Sunday.

Sam liked Newport so much that he encouraged his brother Bud to live there, too. Bud and his wife Audrey moved to the town, where Bud took a job in Sam's store as assistant manager. A few years later, another Ben Franklin store in Versailles, Arkansas, was up for sale. Bud and Sam bought the store as partners, and Bud moved his family to Versailles so he could run the store.

BEATING THE COMPETITION

Although Newport was a small town, Sam's variety store had some tough competition. There was a Sterling variety store right across the street that sold the same merchandise as Sam's Ben Franklin.

The first year Sam was in business, he was outsold by Sterling. Their sales were $170,000 compared to Sam's $80,000.

A clever businessman, Sam would not be outsold for long. He was always looking for a "gimmick" to attract customers. Some of his J.C. Penney-learned methods were as simple as a smile, a personal greeting, knowing customers by name, and helpful service. He would also look for interesting, quality items that were new to the marketplace, like frozen orange juice, for example.

Ice Cream and Popcorn

Among Sam's more elaborate ideas to attract more customers to his store was the purchase of an ice cream machine for $1,250. He set the machine up outside, on the sidewalk in front of the store. When farmers came to town with their families on Saturdays, people lined up to try Sam's fresh ice cream. Although he had to take out a loan to buy the machine, it quickly earned back every dollar he had borrowed . . . and more.

Another attraction that drew customers to Sam's side of the street was a popcorn machine, also set up out front. Strolling shoppers would be lured to the store by the delicious smell of hot popcorn—and hopefully, step inside to buy merchandise as well.

Learning the Value of Taking a Gamble

When a small store next to Sterling became vacant, Sam realized that if his competitor took the space, they would have a big advantage over him. He quickly found the landlord of the empty store and rented it himself.

Having so cleverly outwitted his competition, Sam decided to open what he called a "junior department store" in the empty store. But because it was not much different from a variety store, it did not do well, and Sam closed it down in a few years.

However, Sam learned a valuable lesson from the venture. It was better to try out new ideas and make a mistake than never to take a gamble. Making mistakes did not scare Sam. In his optimistic manner, he believed he could always bounce back from his miscalculation.

As a retailer, Sam was never afraid to make changes, to try new methods, new merchandise, new ideas. A willingness to change, he thought, was the key to improving his store, his sales, and his business. In the Wal-Mart organization today, from top executives to stock clerks, all are encouraged to offer new ideas and suggestions. Wal-Mart calls this philosophy "LTC," or Low Tolerance to Change.

The State's Largest Variety Store

With his ice cream and popcorn machines, Walton was getting a reputation as being somewhat of a circus promoter, but he didn't care. His schemes worked and brought more traffic into his store. Sales grew each year, reaching $225,000 by 1948. Sam beat Sterling that year by $25,000 and was now one of the largest independently owned variety stores in the state.

Sam has also gained a reputation over the years for the special style in which he manages his staff and promotes his stores. When he visits stores—which is quite often—he always has a personal word of praise or encouragement for "associates." He will jump up on a table or check-out counter, take a microphone in hand,

and make an informal speech, praising the staff's work and encouraging them to higher sales in their store.

Sam's style of motivating employees has been compared to that of a Bible-thumping preacher or even a high school cheerleader. The last comparison is not a wild exaggeration. Sam will often lead his famous Wal-Mart cheer ("Give me a W, give me an A, give me an L," etc.) to close his "pep talks."

A KNOCK-OUT BLOW

By 1950 Sam had proven himself a successful merchant, and he looked forward to new ventures. Then, without warning, it seemed that all he had worked so hard to build in Newport was tumbling down around his ears.

Five years earlier, Sam had made a serious error when he negotiated the lease for his store. Now that error was coming back to haunt him. He had failed to insist that the landlord include an option to renew the lease. That meant that when the lease was up in December of 1950, the landlord could then decide whether or not to rent the store to Sam again. What happened was that the landlord saw how profitable the business was that Sam had built. He wanted Sam out so that one of his own sons could run a Ben Franklin on the same property.

Sam could not believe it at first. But then the sad truth set in. After all his hard work, he would have to leave Newport, find a new location, and start all over again. He was heartsick, and most people thought that he was ruined. They did not think that anyone—even plucky Sam Walton—could bounce back after such a knock-out blow.

Chapter 4

No Place to Go . . . But Up!

When Sam Walton lost the lease on his Newport store, he was down but far from out. Ever optimistic, Sam insisted that he could find a new location that would be just as profitable as his busy corner in Newport.

After paying back the $25,000 loan from his father-in-law, Sam had about $50,000 left to **invest** in a new store. He trusted in his special ability to pick profitable locations. He had found Newport that way, and now he scouted around the Arkansas countryside, hoping to stumble upon another hidden gold mine.

AN ALMOST DEAL

The first spot Sam liked was a variety store in Siloam Springs owned by Jim Dodson. The store was beautifully kept, with large windows, freshly painted trim, and a big striped awning that graced the town's main thoroughfare.

With his wife and four children, Sam Walton simply walked into the store one day and told Dodson that he wanted to buy out the business. Understandably, Dodson was shocked and said, "Sorry, this store's not for sale."

Never one to take "no" for an answer, Sam persuaded Dodson to consider the offer. The Waltons stayed in town about four days, and after a few more haggling sessions, the two men came close to an agreement.

Walton offered $60,000 for a package deal—the store and the Dodsons' lovely ten-room house. But Dodson wanted $65,000. Walton would not give in.

Time was running out. In a few months, Sam would be forced out of Newport. But he refused to pay Dodson the extra $5,000. At the time, neither of the men could foresee what the future would bring. Walton would indeed own the Dodson store someday, as part of his large chain. (He and Dodson would also be partners in the hula-hoop episode described earlier.)

At that moment, however, although on the verge of losing his store in Newport, Sam still would not give in to Dodson's demand for the extra $5,000. Gathering his determination and whatever pioneer grit he had inherited from his forefathers, Sam packed up his family and left Siloam Springs.

ON TO BENTONVILLE

About a week or so later, Sam found another possible store location in Bentonville, Arkansas. The store was a Ben Franklin owned by seventy-year-old Luther Harrison. The Butler Brothers told Walton that the store was not officially for sale, but Harrison might be ready to retire after twenty-six years of shopkeeping.

Walton went to Bentonville with his father-in-law to look the store and town over. Harrison Variety was the complete opposite of Jim Dodson's polished jewel of a store. It was dark, dusty, and out of date. Mr. Robson was not impressed and wanted to go home.

But Walton took a more imaginative view. He thought the store's location on the main square was promising. He also wondered if he could get the neighboring barbershop. This would double the store's scant twenty-five foot frontage to fifty feet.

Making a Deal

It did not take much to persuade Luther Harrison to retire. A deal was soon struck for $15,000 for the store, merchandise, and fixtures. However, Harrison did not own the property. He just rented it for $25 a month. Wary of another lease problem, Walton insisted that he wanted to buy the entire building and get a ninety-nine-year lease on the barbershop next door. Or else, no deal.

After some tense negotiations including the help of Mr. Robson, the people who owned the property were persuaded to sell. Mr. Robson was doubtful about the whole deal, but Walton convinced him that everything would work out. He would do the same things in Bentonville that he had done in Newport. Maybe even better.

STARTING OVER

Sam Walton took possession of the Bentonville store the first week in May of 1950. A record rainfall of twelve inches in twenty-four hours turned the opening day into a soggy, disheartening event.

This Wal-Mart Visitors Center is located in the store that Sam Walton opened in Bentonville, Arkansas, in May of 1950. (Benton County Daily Democrat.)

Water poured through the old roof and ruined merchandise that couldn't be covered quickly enough. The old store needed renovations . . . and fast.

But Sam had a way of taking the lemons in his life and making lemonade. He attracted customers soon after the opening with a "Remodeling Sale." He modernized the store with bigger windows, new lighting, and shelves. For the first time, he hung a sign outside the store that said, "Walton's 5¢ & 10¢." But the cost of the store and remodeling it had used up his $50,000. Starting off fresh, Sam was "down to zero again."

Walton kept his store in Newport open until the end of his lease in December of 1950 and ran the two stores simultaneously. It was a hectic time for him. Sad news came in late September when Sam learned that his mother had cancer. She entered a hospital in St. Louis for an operation and died a few days later.

A Different Town

Bentonville was somewhat different from Newport. The Waltons soon learned that traditions and history in this town ran deep. The residents were friendly and easy-going, but were not quite as accepting of newcomers as the folks in Newport had been. To do business successfully in Bentonville, Sam had to learn about the local customs.

Nevertheless, the Waltons liked Bentonville very much, enough to make it their permanent home and eventually build a three-bedroom house there in 1959. The Waltons still live in the same house, despite the fact that they could certainly buy or build a far grander home.

During the early months of the transition from Newport to Bentonville, Sam realized that it was hard work to run more than one store at a time. But he also realized that it could indeed be done. He drove a great deal during those months, an eight-hour trip between the two stores. And he would often drive 200 miles to the Butler Brothers' warehouse in Kansas City.

Walton was already visualizing a chain of variety stores. But he knew he could never manage them effectively with no better means of transportation than his car. However, always a good problem solver, he thought he could do it if he learned how to fly a plane.

A TALENT FOR EXPANSION

Sam was eager to open more stores. He would drive around the small towns near Bentonville to check out possible new locations. He also inquired at the Butler Brothers' headquarters if any Ben Franklin franchises were for sale. He would sit in town squares and watch the traffic on the shopping thoroughfares. More traffic meant more shoppers. And he looked for growing towns located near main highways, or near highway intersections for easy access.

Sam would also count cars parked at town squares—a habit that his friends and family would eventually joke about. (Once he was so engrossed counting the cars in the parking lot of one of his stores that he drove right into the back of a huge Wal-Mart delivery truck.)

Taking a look around Fayetteville, Arkansas, a town about twenty-five miles south of Bentonville, Sam liked what he saw. There was lots of traffic in the main square, and the town was located on a direct highway route to Kansas City. When he learned that the grocery store on the square was closing, Sam quickly took over the lease.

Chapter 5

Growing Pains

When the Fayetteville store opened in October of 1952, Sam hired Willard Walker, from Tulsa, Oklahoma, to be the manager. Now that he had been bitten by the expansion bug, Sam knew that he not only needed to find good store locations, but good managers to run them.

In order to motivate them, Sam offered a percentage of the store's profits to the managers. He and his managers cut the cost of running the stores by doing a great deal of the work themselves, such as setting up **displays,** laying floor tile, painting, cleaning, and transporting merchandise. The new managers had to be willing to put in long hours, but they didn't mind since they were receiving a share of their store's profits. Sam has continued to be a strong believer in the practice of sharing Wal-Mart's profits with company employees.

THE SHOPPING CENTER VENTURE

The next location Sam found was in Ruskin Heights, a suburb of Kansas City. This location was somewhat different from Sam's other two stores. It was a spot in the second shopping center ever built in the United States. At that time, some people had their doubts that shopping centers would be more profitable locations than those on a traditional main street. But Sam's instincts told him that this was the future for retailers.

Sam and Bud again became partners in the Ruskin Heights store. However, not even Sam could guess how remarkably profitable the store would be. Within three years, annual sales were $350,000, about $150,000 more than any of his or Bud's other stores.

A Lost Investment

Sam Walton was amazed by the profits from his store in the Ruskin Heights shopping center. He began scouting the outskirts of towns again. This time, however, he was not looking for merely a new store location. Instead, he wanted to find a large parcel of land where he could build his own shopping center.

Walton knew that he could not finance such a large venture on his own. But he hoped that if he found a good location, he could interest other investors.

Sam found a spot in Little Rock and put down a deposit of $10,000 to buy the land. He had big ideas about developing shopping centers all over. "I thought it was a cinch," he said once, looking back.

However, there was more to the business of developing a shopping center than Sam—with all of his optimism and positive thinking—had figured on. During the next few months, he invested over $25,000 in the Little Rock project but found himself still a long way from completion. Finally, he decided to give up on the venture, even though it meant losing his investment. Sometime later, he said, "We had big ideas, but no money."

Sam settled for leasing a store for another five-and-ten in Little Rock. However, his initial instinct was right. Later, someone else did develop a successful shopping center at the same location he had chosen.

A HOTSHOT PILOT

Sam now turned his attention back to finding more locations for his five-and-tens. He had learned how to fly and found the new freedom and speed ideal for checking out new properties.

Instead of driving, Sam would now swoop around the countryside in a plane, getting a bird's-eye view of new housing developments, trailer parks, and towns. He would load his plane with merchandise or even his hunting dogs, visiting all his stores in one day and then taking a few hours out for "a hunting break." (Sam was prone to take such breaks like other businessmen take coffee breaks.)

Even today, Sam and his key Wal-Mart executives use the same technique to oversee their vast operations. They "hop" from town to town in the corporate plane, visiting several Wal-Mart locations in one day. For a time, one of Sam's sons even served as the corporate pilot.

Making Passengers Nervous

Walton estimates that he has logged about 10,000 hours as a pilot and traveled about 1.5 million miles in over forty years aloft. His brother Bud, a former Navy pilot, did not have much confidence in Sam's flying at the start. He thought Sam was a reckless pilot and his first plane unsafe.

Sam has been called a "slapdash" or "careless" pilot, but he's never had a serious accident. He can sometimes make passengers nervous, however, when he puts the plane on automatic control and starts reading maps or gazing out the window for new store locations. He's often been known to comfort nervous passengers with the phrase, "Don't worry, it's a big sky out there."

FAMILY AND FORTUNE

During the late 1950s, Sam worked long hours building his chain of five-and-ten stores. But he also took time out for his hobbies—hunting and tennis, for family camping vacations, serving as a church deacon, and for civic organizations, such as the Rotary Club and chamber of commerce.

During the early days in Bentonville, as the Walton fortune was growing, Sam and Helen were concerned about teaching their children the value of hard work and careful handling of money. As the children grew, they took such part-time jobs as paper routes, babysitting, and working in their father's stores, where they stocked the shelves or operated the popcorn machine. They were paid for their time, just like any other employee. They also paid for any merchandise they wanted from the store, just like any other customer.

But when the Walton children finished college and chose careers, the family business did not interest any of them. In later years, however, Rob, Jim, and Alice have become more involved in various aspects of Wal-Mart and investing the family billions.

From 1985 to 1989, Sam was named the richest man in America by *Forbes* magazine. His personal fortune was estimated at $9 billion. However, soon after opening his first store, Sam had a legal document drawn up which divided his money equally between himself, his wife, and his chidren. Therefore, when Forbes later learned about this, they included the entire Walton family together in their list of rich Americans. But now they were much farther down the list, as their wealth was estimated at about 1.8 billion dollars each.

THE FIRST BIG STORE

By the late 1950s, there were eleven Walton five-and-tens in operation. However, Sam and Bud did not have all the money necessary to open new stores on their own. So they devised various ways to raise capital. In a 1987 interview for *Wal-Mart World*, a corporate newsletter, they talked about this period of growth.

> All the stores were opened under different arrangements. It was a collection of partnerships and individual ownerships . . . including all the store managers who could raise money to invest.

About this time, Sam spotted a promising new town, St. Robert, Arkansas. However, there was no space available in the town to rent for a new store. But Bud, who was handling most of the real estate deals at that time, found a grocer who was building a supermarket.

He talked the man into making a larger building and allowing the Waltons to lease part of it.

An Outstanding Success

The store started out at 13,000 square feet, but in a year it was expanded to 20,000 square feet. Sales were outstanding right from the start—$2 million per year. Once again, Sam's talent for picking great locations had paid off big.

The store in St. Robert was an important step in the building of the Wal-Mart idea. It showed that a big store could work, and its success inspired Sam with even grander, more ambitious ideas. Of that store's success, Bud has said, "It showed what the potential was for high-volume sales and probably gave Sam the idea of just how far he could go."

LEARNING ABOUT DISCOUNTING

Sam Walton never tired of studying his competitors and adopting new ways to improve his own business. "If they had something good," he once said of his competitors, "we copied it."

At the very start of the 1960s, Sam became fascinated with a new concept in retailing called discount stores. He traveled to all the new stores of this kind and talked to company executives, store managers, clerks, and even customers. He studied the store layouts, displays, and **pricing**, jotting down notes on a little pad. One merchant later described Sam as someone who was "always asking questions and trying to learn."

Sam Walton probably never dreamed in the 1950s that his small five-and-tens would some day become a mammoth chain of stores that would include this gigantic superstore near Dallas, Texas. (Bob Byrd.)

Cumberland, Rhode Island, was one of Sam's first stops. He wanted to see the Ann & Hope discount outlet, one of the first low-overhead, self-service stores of its kind. The store was set up in 5,000 square feet of a deserted textile mill.

At that time, the S.S. Kresge Company, which operated variety stores similar to the Ben Franklin chain, was also interested in the discount store concept. Harry Cunningham of Kresge studied Ann & Hope and came up with the plan for K-Mart stores. Sam watched K-Mart closely.

As he continued roaming New England from 1960 to 1962, Sam started forming his own plans. He had less time now for local activities and civic affairs. His Bentonville friends noticed his absence from town meetings and the Horseshoe Cafe, where they would talk over local news and politics.

"Where was Sam these days?" they wondered. "What sort of wild, new business scheme was he trying to hatch now?"

Chapter 6

The Wal-Mart Idea

In 1962, Sam traveled to Chicago to meet with the top executives at the Butler Brothers Corporation. He proposed the idea of Ben Franklin discount stores. The stores would be franchised, like the five-and-tens, and located in rural markets. In those locations, the stores would not face heavy competition from chains like K-Mart. Walton told the gathering of executives that he would be willing to gamble his money on the experiment as the first franchise owner.

A REJECTED PROPOSAL

Butler Brothers' executives could see that discount stores were on the rise. However, Sam Walton told them that in order for the plan to work, the company would have to cut in half the profits made on the wholesale goods they sold to franchise owners. Instead of making 20 percent to 25 percent profit, they'd be making only 12.5

percent. The volume of sales, Sam explained, would more than make up for the lower profits.

"Cut profits in *half?*" The executives were outraged. Some thought Sam's proposal was crazy.

"No thanks, Mr. Walton," the executives at Butler Brothers told Sam. "We don't think your discount outlet idea is for us. Goodbye . . . and good luck."

Still Learning

Sam headed back to Bentonville, but first he stopped at a K-Mart in a Chicago suburb. As he crouched under a display counter, notepad in hand, he heard one of the Butler Brothers' executives, Donald Soderquist, call his name.

"Mr. Walton, what are you doing?" Soderquist asked Sam.

"Just part of the education process, Don. I'm still learning," Walton replied.

Naturally, Sam was sorry that Butler Brothers hadn't agreed to his proposal. But their rejection did not make Walton give up on his idea. If Butler Brothers didn't want to franchise discount stores, he would figure out some other way to get them started.

As for Donald Soderquist, he was impressed by Sam's persistence. About ten years later, he took a job as a top executive at Wal-Mart.

THE FIRST WAL-MART

Sam scouted around for other partners and other possibilities. Finally, with the financial backing of the Republic National Bank in Dallas, Texas, Sam was able to open his first discount outlet, which he called Wal-Mart, in Rogers, Arkansas.

The first Wal-Mart opened in 1962 in a new building that offered about 16,000 square feet of space. It was not very large compared to later stores. By all accounts, it was not much to look at inside either, even after the merchandise was set up and the doors opened.

As the store manager, Clarence Leis has recalled, the first Wal-Mart had no shelves, only tables and a few racks. Items were not arranged or displayed, "just put there like a big sale."

At the start, Walton and his managers could only stock low- and medium-quality merchandise. This was because many manufacturers would not sell to a discounter whose **merchandising** method and "no frills" setting they thought "cheapened" their product. In time, however, Walton and his staff were able to upgrade the quality of their merchandise as manufacturers began to accept the Wal-Mart idea.

"A Copying Proposition"

Those first months, Leis did his best to arrange items in a more orderly way, with Walton hovering around like an anxious mother hen. The store did a good business from the start, making about $700,000 in sales the first year.

Sam has often explained that he modeled Wal-Mart mainly after the K-Mart stores. "What I did . . . was take pieces of it [K-Mart] and make Wal-Mart as much like it as we could. It was a copying proposition." He has described the early Wal-Marts as "amateurish and far behind" K-Mart. Today, however, Walton reports that K-Mart is now copying Wal-Mart stores.

Even after Sam opened more Wal-Marts, K-Mart did not consider the tiny chain serious competition. Walton's strategy was to

stick to rural locations, out of K-Mart's territory in the more popu-
lated urban and suburban areas.

A GRAND OPENING MESS

While the "kinks" in the first Wal-Mart store were being worked out,
Sam was already arranging the opening of his second outlet in
Harrison, Arkansas, eighty miles east of Rogers. Sam found a good
location in early summer of 1964 and the store was opened by
mid-August.

The grand opening of the Harrison Wal-Mart was another
Walton extravaganza. There was a donkey to give kiddie rides out in
the parking lot. And there was a pile of watermelons, free for
customers. However, Harrison was in the middle of a heat wave, and
the temperature on the day of the grand opening hit 115 degrees.
By the end of the day, the watermelons had exploded, mixing with
the donkey droppings, making an unsightly mess.

An Error in Judgment

The scene did not make a good impression on David Glass, a young
executive with the Cranks Drug Company. Sam had invited Glass to
the Grand Opening as part of his campaign to persuade Glass to
work for Wal-Mart. As Glass recalls the day, "He was a nice fellow,
but I wrote him off. It was just terrible."

Some years later, Glass would have a far different impression
of Sam and Wal-Mart. He would eventually join the firm and
become its **chief executive officer (CEO)**. He readily admits now
that he totally misjudged Sam's persistence and his capacity for
improvement.

By 1966, the third Wal-Mart had opened in Siloam Springs and the fourth in Springdale. Sam and his partners also had eighteen Ben Franklin stores in operation.

BUILDING A STAFF

Sam now faced several key problems in expanding the Wal-Mart chain. One was the ongoing problem of financing, which he had faced while expanding his five-and-ten chain of Ben Franklin stores. Another was buying merchandise at the lowest possible wholesale prices.

Sam had always shown a talent for picking good store managers to run the five-and-tens, but now he needed more than on-site managers. He needed to find sharp, ambitious executives who would help him build the Wal-Mart chain and solve its many problems. He not only looked for such people at big companies, he also looked within his own staff for any imaginative, talented store managers he could promote.

A Belief in the Future

Sam went to great lengths to persuade the men he wanted to come to work for Wal-Mart, sometimes "wooing" them for as long as a year. But leaving a big, well-established company to take a job with a small, new chain was a tremendous gamble. Walton tried to convince the men he hoped to hire that they'd have a great opportunity and big future if they helped build his new enterprise.

Some of the people Walton hired at this time had already

tried to persuade the companies they were with to open discount outlets. They liked Sam's adventurous, foresighted approach and believed Wal-Mart had a good future.

GROWING BIGGER

Along with his new staff, Walton set about solving the many day-to-day and long-term problems that his new chain was having.

In 1968, only six years after the not-so-grand opening of the first Wal-Marts, the chain had twenty-four stores in operation with annual sales of $12.5 million. At this time, Sam built new corporate headquarters in Bentonville. He kept the office space as small as possible but built a vast warehouse of 60,000 square feet. The warehouse was a distribution center where merchandise for his stores could be transported quickly and efficiently in Wal-Mart's own fleet of trucks.

Other retail chains usually build their warehouses near existing stores. Sam, however, built his huge warehouse first, then found sites for new stores around it, within 300 miles or a five- to six-hour truck drive. On a map, the new warehouse was the center of a circle, with possible new Wal-Mart stores located 300 miles or less in any direction.

Keys to Success

Within three years, both the office and warehouse space at Wal-Mart headquarters were doubled to accommodate the larger staff and many new stores. The warehouse was now the size of about three football fields.

The Wal-Mart Distribution Centers

The average Wal-Mart distribution center covers about thirty acres and contains 1.2 million square feet of space. Part of the space is for storage, other parts are for loading and unloading goods. The center is connected by about eleven miles of conveyor belts. Controlled by scanners, the belts carry goods out of storage, down ramps, and into delivery trucks, also owned by Wal-Mart. The belts may carry as many as 190,000 cases of goods each day.

Approximately 1,000 "associates" work at a center, some loading or unloading as many as 300 trucks of merchandise daily. The center services about 150 to 200 stores, most located within a single day's drive.

As the chain grew in the area around Bentonville, some exceptions to the 300-mile limit were made. However, once Wal-Mart decided to expand outside of the Bentonville area, new distribution centers were built to serve new store clusters.

The principle of placing stores close to distribution centers and the constant improvement of operating systems at these centers proved to be important factors to Wal-Mart's success. In an interview with Fortune magazine, David Glass, Wal-Mart's CEO, said, "Our distribution facilities are one of the keys to our success. If we do anything better than the other folks, that's it."

GOING PUBLIC

With a dynamic team in place, Sam set big goals for the number of new Wal-Mart stores he wanted to open each year. By 1969, annual sales had increased to a little over $21.3 million, an impressive leap over the $12.5 million in 1968 by any standards. Along with Ron Mayer, Wal-Mart's new chief financial officer, Sam planned that in six years—by 1975—the Wal-Mart chain would hit $230 million annually in sales.

Such an increase would be over one hundred times the 1969 sales volume. It sounded unbelievable to some business experts. They thought Walton was far beyond being optimistic—just plain pie-in-the-sky crazy to believe his company could grow at that rate.

Until this time, Sam had relied on banks, partners, and loans from large insurance companies to finance the expansion of Wal-Mart. But those sources were no longer reliable enough for his ambitious, long-term plans. So, to raise the money he needed to pursue his plans, in 1969 Sam decided to "go public"—that is, make Wal-Mart a publicly owned company—by selling **shares of stock** in the company. An offering of 300,000 shares of Wal-Mart, at $16.50 per share, would raise about $5 million.

The stock was finally offered in October 1970. Investors who had heard about Wal-Mart's impressive growth so far eagerly bought the stock. It proved to be a terrific investment. Over the next twenty years, the stock split two-for-one (two new shares given by the company for every one share a person already owns) several times. An investment of $1,650 for 100 shares of Wal-Mart stock in 1970 would have grown to 25,000 shares and be worth over $1 million by 1990!

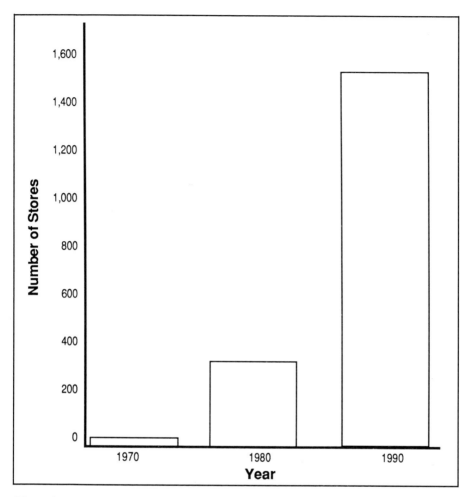

This chart illustrates the explosive growth in the number of Wal-Mart stores in just twenty years, from 38 in 1970 to over 1,500 by 1990.

TURNING DREAMS INTO REALITY

Up until this point, Sam Walton's "targets" and corporate goals were just so many statistics on paper. Now, with the capital needed to expand in hand, Sam began to turn his ambitious paper dreams into reality.

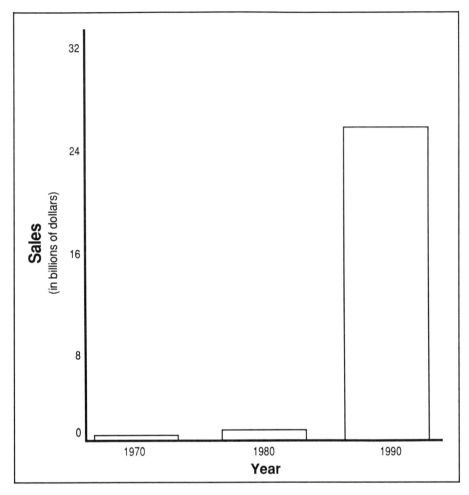

In the twenty-year period from 1970 to 1990, Wal-Mart's annual sales increased from $30 million to almost $26 billion, a fantastic growth by any standard of measure.

One year after going public, there were fifty-one Wal-Mart stores in operation. The chain now stretched from Arkansas to Missouri, Kansas, Oklahoma, and Louisiana. Sales for 1971 were over $78 million.

Despite the disbelievers Sam had met in 1968, by 1975 the Wal-Mart chain did reach his goal of $230 million in total sales. Reached it . . . and exceeded it by $6 million!

Chapter 7

Public Victories, Private Challenges

In 1974, Sam Walton looked at the booming Wal-Mart empire he had created and considered his future. At age fifty-six, he had worked as a retail merchant for about thirty years. At the expense of spending time with his wife and children, he had devoted the best part of the last twelve years of his life to building his Wal-Mart dream.

It now seemed to Sam that perhaps the greater part of his work was done. Perhaps it was time for him to step aside, slow down, and enjoy some of the rewards of his hard-won success.

PICKING A SUCCESSOR

It was clear by now that none of Sam's four children or his brother Bud had an interest in taking over as the head of Wal-Mart. So Ron Mayer, the company's chief financial officer, was the likely choice as Sam's successor.

Mayer had joined Wal-Mart in 1969 and had worked side-by-side with Sam to take the company public, to set goals for the chain's growth, and to meet those goals. Because Mayer was also quite ambitious, Sam worried that if he did not give him the top job at Wal-Mart soon, the company would lose its most talented executive to another organization.

Stepping Aside

Sam made a difficult and important decision in 1974. He announced that he would retire and give Mayer the top job at Wal-Mart. From now on, Sam would only play a sideline role in running the company. However, he would still hold a large chunk of the company's stock and would serve on the **board of directors** and as chairman of the **executive committee.**

It seemed like a sound plan. Mayer was both liked and respected by almost everyone who worked for him or knew him through the retailing field. He was only forty years old and considered a "boy wonder" of retailing.

A SHORT RETIREMENT

Sam now began spending more time perfecting his tennis serve, flying his plane, and hunting. He also had more time for Bentonville civic affairs and other business ventures, such as buying part share in the new First National Bank of Rogers.

Yet, although on the sidelines, Sam was still in his office at Wal-Mart headquarters almost every day, and still swooping around nine states in his plane to visit Wal-Mart stores like a guardian angel. If he didn't like something he saw or thought of an improvement for the chain, he usually didn't wait to tell Mayer about it, but simply corrected the problem on his own. This was clearly infringing on Mayer's authority, but Sam couldn't seem to help it.

Mayer Resigns

It soon became clear to all involved that Sam Walton was not yet ready to retire. Sam himself realized that he had made a mistake, but it was a sticky situation to correct. In the spring of 1976, only twenty months after he had "crowned" Mayer CEO, Sam asked Mayer to step back to the post of chief financial officer, his previous job. Sam wanted to be back in charge at Wal-Mart again.

Mayer, however, did not want to return to his former job, so he resigned from the company. Sam was sorry to see Mayer go. In many interviews he has emphasized his high regard for Mayer and the important contributions he made to Wal-Mart's growth during his five years with the company.

The changes going on in Wal-Mart's headquarters did not look good to outsiders, especially to financial experts. The price of Wal-Mart stock went down at this time because the company leadership looked so unstable.

The drop, however, was only temporary. Sam was now back at the helm and pushing the Wal-Mart throttle full-speed ahead. In 1977, the company's **annual report** to stockholders showed sales at $478.8 million for 153 stores in nine states. Sam also announced a new goal for Wal-Mart: to become a billion-dollar company within four years.

PEAKS AND VALLEYS

The early 1980s was a difficult period for Sam Walton, his company, and his entire family. He faced several challenges in Wal-Mart's next phase of growth and in his private life as well.

The Wal-Mart Distribution System

The process of moving merchandise from the manufacturer to the consumer is called distribution. When discount chains like Wal-Mart were just starting, wholesalers (the people who represent manufacturers and supply retailers) did not service small, rural communities. For this reason, Wal-Mart was forced to develop its own distribution system, the basics of which are as follows.

At each store, check-out scanners read the bar coding on items to keep track of sales and the supply of products on the shelves. The stores send merchandise orders through the company's satellite communications system to the main computer at corporate headquarters in Bentonville. The main computer, in turn, constantly monitors product inventory levels at Wal-Mart's many distribution centers and sends orders to manufacturers whenever necessary. Some manufacturers are even hooked up directly to the Wal-Mart computer and can anticipate the company's needs.

Orders from a store are quickly transferred by the satellite communications system to the store's nearest Wal-Mart distribution center. Merchandise from the center is then delivered to the store in a Wal-Mart truck, usually within thirty-six hours after the store sent in its order.

In the late 1970s the company had begun to computerize its operations with a $500 million plan that would take about five years to complete. The main computer was located in Bentonville and hooked into all Wal-Mart stores, warehouses, and distribution centers. Sam was wary at first of entering the new computer age, but he could soon see the tremendous benefits in terms of time saved and more efficient operations.

In 1980, Wal-Mart hit its billion-dollar sales goal. During the next few years, however, Wal-Mart ran into a few rough waves in its sailing. Sam and his top executives calculated profit targets, but the chain did not meet those goals.

Walton was determined to find out what had gone wrong in his stores and fix it. Also, competitors were beginning to move into Wal-Mart's territory.

To improve sales and beat the competition, changes were made in Wal-Mart's entire **marketing** strategy. Stores were redecorated to make them more comfortable and attractive to shoppers. Cheaper merchandise was abandoned in favor of high-quality, name brands. Sam not only appealed to Wal-Mart's top executives for suggestions on improving the company, but took ideas from all his associates, from vice-presidents to stock clerks.

A Dreaded Disease

In the late summer of 1982, as Sam struggled to keep Wal-Mart on a successful track, he found his normal schedule exhausting. He was now sixty-four years old. Perhaps it was time to slow down his pace, Sam told himself. But a lighter work schedule and less time on the tennis court and in hunting fields did little to improve his energy level. Finally, Sam had a complete physical examination.

The news was devastating. Sam was soon diagnosed with hairy cell leukemia. Known as HCL, this type of leukemia is a cancer of the blood that destroys the body's white blood cells. With fewer white blood cells, the body has difficulty fighting infections. A minor cold can be fatal.

In October 1982, Sam went to the M.D. Anderson Hospital in Houston, Texas, one of the country's leading cancer-treatment centers. He learned there that he had a few choices of treatment, none of which appealed to him. Then he met Dr. Jorge R. Quesada, who was experimenting with a method of treating HCL with a drug called interferon.

Taking a Gamble

Several types of cancer were being treated successfully with interferon, but Dr. Quesada made it clear to Sam that only ten patients so far had taken interferon for HCL. He warned Sam that the treatment would be a gamble. The drug might not work, and some side effects were perhaps still unknown.

It was a difficult decision, but the gambler and pioneer spirit in Sam Walton pushed him to try the experimental drug instead of the more traditional treatments. Sam learned how to give himself daily shots of interferon, much in the same way as a diabetic receives insulin. He carried out the daily therapy for six months, then switched to a schedule of three times a week.

Miraculously, in a few months' time, Sam's cancer was in remission—an inactive state. The threat of HCL becoming active again would always linger in the shadows, but Sam felt his former strength and energy return. The gamble paid off big. Sam won his fight against HCL and no sign of the disease has recurred.

A SALUTE FROM BENTONVILLE

Well on the road to recovery from HCL, Sam was cheered by a salute from the citizens of Bentonville. On October 8, 1983, the town honored the entire Walton family with an Appreciation Day. Sam Walton's company had virtually put Bentonville on the map. His corporation had brought jobs and commerce to the area, and both Sam and Helen had given generously of their time to Bentonville's community.

For all these reasons and many more, the town's leading citizens received many honors that day. There was a parade up the main street and a show with Grand Old Opry stars, bluegrass music, and a college choir. The town's junior high school was renamed in Sam's honor, and its daycare center dedicated to Helen. Even a street was renamed "Walton Boulevard."

A Message from the President

The entire celebration peaked that night with a huge banquet attended by 1,200 guests. Sam and Helen were showered with plaques and congratulatory speeches. Even President Ronald Reagan telephoned. "I want to pay a special tribute to the both of you for being an outstanding example of those principles of dedication, hard work, free enterprise, and the spirit that has made this nation great and strong," the President said.

Deeply moved, Sam replied to his night of honors with tears in his eyes. "You people should not be thanking us," he said. "We should be thanking you for all the support you have given us through these thirty years."

Chapter 8

Taking Wal-Mart to the Top

Perhaps the most striking example of Sam's dedication to American principles of free enterprise, as cited by President Reagan, is his "Buy American" campaign. The campaign started in answer to a pressing problem with the American economy. Throughout the 1970s, retailers had been buying increasing amounts of foreign-made goods because the prices were cheaper. But turning to foreign manufacturers for merchandise often put American factories out of business.

A GOVERNOR'S REQUEST FOR HELP

In 1984, the governor of Arkansas called Sam regarding this problem. Farris Burroughs, a clothing manufacturer in Brinkley, was about to go out of business. He had been producing flannel shirts that were sold by Van Husen in J.C. Penney and Sears stores. Now Van Husen was giving the work to a company in China and Burroughs might have to close his factory, which employed ninety people.

Sam Walton promised the governor that he'd try to think of some way to help. Wal-Mart was also buying most of its flannel shirts overseas. But Sam was determined to give Burroughs a large enough order to keep him in business.

After working out some problems, Wal-Mart gave Burroughs a contract for 240,000 shirts at $612,000. The sewing machines at Burroughs' factory began humming again and his staff more than doubled.

PROMOTING THE "BUY AMERICAN" PLAN

Although the "Buy American" program required a reduction in Wal-Mart's profits, it was not enough to convince Sam that the venture was not worthwhile. He was so impressed with the success of the Burroughs experiment that he sent a letter to 3,000 American manufacturers and wholesalers explaining his "Buy American" plan and urging them to join him in his effort to save American jobs.

But other companies were reluctant to take up Walton's fight against foreign manufacturers. Some claimed that Sam's plan was primarily a publicity stunt. Wal-Mart, however, expanded its efforts, seeking out American manufacturers to produce items that it had been buying overseas, from patio chairs to children's T-shirts.

In 1986, Wal-Mart invited the press and executives from other companies to a conference in Little Rock. Sam enthusiastically showed off the items that Wal-Mart now sold as part of the "Buy American" campaign. He claimed that in that past year, the program had created or restored 4,583 jobs in the United States.

A Great Loss

In August of 1984, Sam had to face another hard emotional blow. His father Tom died at age ninety-two. Sam had always been close to his father and visited him regularly, once a month, in Columbia. In 1982, Sam even had his father cut the ribbon at a special store opening in the family's old hometown of Kingfisher, Oklahoma.

Sam was so saddened by the loss of his father that he went into a depression that lasted for several weeks. One way he chose to honor his father's memory was by donating, along with Bud, $150,000 for a new Columbia Chamber of Commerce Convention and Visitors Bureau, called the Thomas G. Walton Building. In memory of his father, Sam took Tom's favorite walking stick and hung it on the wall of his office, where it hangs to this day.

WHOLESALE CLUBS

Sam's roaming around New England in the early 1960s, trying to learn all about the new retail ventures called discount stores, paid off. He learned so well that by 1980 Wal-Mart had 330 stores and annual sales of $1.2 billion. But was Sam satisfied? Did he ever consider his retailing education over? Not Samuel Moore Walton!

Twenty years later, in 1982, Sam traveled to the West Coast to investigate a new type of discount store called a wholesale club. The wholesale club concept had been invented by Sol Price, a

Wal-Mart is meeting its competition head on. At the start of 1990, Wal-Mart was the third largest retailer in the country, behind Sears and K-Mart, respectively, in terms of numbers of stores in operation and total dollar sales.

But Wal-Mart surpassed its rivals in profits earned during 1988 and 1989. It has also continued to show a faster rate of growth. Sam's new goal is to see Wal-Mart on top, in the number-one spot in total sales and number of stores. Many business experts predict that it won't be long.

Will Sam Walton be leading his company to this coveted position? He tried retiring once, but that didn't quite work out as planned. In February of 1988, Sam named David Glass as Wal-Mart's new CEO. But he retained the position of chairman of the board of directors and remains active in all phases of running Wal-Mart.

Another Health Crisis

Amid the excitement of Wal-Mart's surge into new market areas, Sam again faced a serious health crisis. In November of 1989, he was told by his doctors in Houston that another kind of cancer had been found in his body. This time, seven years after his bout with HCL, Sam was diagnosed with cancer of the bone marrow. Unlike HCL, this type of cancer has no cure or treatment to easily control its spread.

Sam has endured the available treatment of chemotherapy (taking of drugs) and radiation, which have brought on many painful side effects. The pain from the disease itself has been severe. Yet, when he was questioned by a reporter, Sam's optimism persisted. "I've got a good chance to recover," he said, "a sixty percent chance, at least with the type of medicine I'm getting. So I think things are fine."

During his chemotherapy treatments, Walton left the hospital for a short visit to a local Sam's Wholesale Club. He also spent a weekend in Bentonville to attend the standard Saturday morning staff meeting of store managers, buyers, and department heads. There is no keeping Sam down.

In the spring of 1990, the fight continued to be hard, but Sam still managed to visit his office almost every day and maintain an active interest in even the smallest detail of running the giant Wal-Mart chain. Sam is now his own greatest challenge, but he simply refuses to be beaten.

WAL-MART 2000

What does Sam Walton foresee for the future of Wal-Mart? To a gathering of 9,000 employees, investors, and news media, Sam presented his predictions at the University of Arkansas campus on June 1, 1990.

He predicted that by the year 2000, the retailing empire he had founded with one five-and-ten-cent store would have over 3,000 discount stores and wholesale outlets in operation, doing $129 billion in business each year.

Sam's prediction may be optimistic, but as he so often has said, "It's a big sky out there."

Glossary

annual report A report on the finances of a company made to its stockholders at the end of each year; includes such information as profits or losses for the year, improvements in operations, and plans and goals for the future.

board of directors A group of people who run the affairs of a company for those who own stock in it.

capital Money, goods, or property used to produce income.

chief executive officer (CEO) A company's highest ranking decision-maker.

discount To reduce the price of an item; often used in regard to prices that are lower than the list price (the manufacturer's suggested retail price).

displays The ways in which items in a store are arranged on shelves or in windows in order to attract customers.

distributor An organization or individual who buys items in large quantities from a manufacturer, then sells the items to retail stores for sale to the consumer.

executive committee A group of people who manage the operations of a company.

franchise The right given to an individual or a group to sell a company's goods or services in a particular area.

Great Depression A period during the 1930s of low economic activity in the United States, with much unemployment.

gross profits The total amount of earnings before expenses are subtracted.

invest To put money or capital into a business venture in order to gain profit or growth in the future.

marketing The advertising and selling of products or services by companies.

merchandise The goods that are bought and sold by a store.

merchandising The specific way items are sold in regard to such factors as setting, display, pricing, and service.

mortgage A real estate loan that generally covers an extended number of years.

overhead All operating expenses of a business, such as rent, salaries, and cost of goods.

pricing The process of deciding the price at which to sell an item; involves marking up or adding to the wholesale cost of an item to cover overhead costs and make a profit.

profits The money left over from selling goods or services after all expenses are subtracted; also considered the net revenue or net gain.

retailing The selling of goods to the general public.

self-service A type of merchandising in which customers select items without the aid of a salesperson and then pay for them at a check-out counter.

shares of stock Certificates showing part ownership in a company or corporation.

variety store One that sells many different kinds of small items.

wholesale The sale of goods in large quantities, usually for resale by a retailer.

Index